MW00683315

TOASTS
for Any
OCCASION

new seasons®

Original toasts by **Ellen F. Pill, Ph.D., Paul Seaburn,** and **Jennifer John Ouellette.**
Ellen F. Pill is a contributing editor for *Discovery Girls* magazine and author of *Everybody Gets Angry.*
Her work has appeared in *Church Chuckles, Teens' Guide for a Purposeful Life,* and other publications.
Paul Seaburn, head writer for *Taylor's Attic,* creates radio comedy scripts and teaches comedy. His
work has appeared in *From the Horse's Mouth, Tales From the Teacher's Lounge,* and other publications.
Jennifer John Ouellette is an award-winning radio journalist and freelance writer. Her work has
appeared in *When You Need the Right Words, Prayers for Our Country,* and other publications.

Illustrations by **Lynda Calvert-Weyant.**

New Seasons is a registered trademark of Publications International, Ltd.

Louis Weber, CEO
Publications International, Ltd.
7373 N. Cicero Avenue
Lincolnwood, Illinois 60712

www.pilbooks.com

Manufactured in China.

8 7 6 5 4 3 2 1

ISBN-13: 978-1-4127-5404-0

ISBN-10: 1-4127-5404-6

CONTENTS

INTRODUCTION

A JOKE IS JUST A JOKE, A QUIP IS JUST A QUIP, a bon mot is . . . well, no one really knows what a bon mot is. However, a well-prepared toast can turn the lifting of a drink into a lasting memory. On special occasions, a toast can provide the most unforgettable words after "I do," "Good luck," and "The drinks are on me." For those who want to master the art of the toast, *Toasts for Any Occasion* is just the ticket.

A good toast can be serious or funny, light or thought provoking, loving or roasting. But to make that good toast into a great one, you need one more thing: brevity. Don't let your toast last longer than the ice in your glass. You want your audience to remember what you said, not how long it took you to say it.

Keep in mind that a good toast should match the occasion. Newlyweds drink to a new beginning, while a couple celebrating 50 years together drinks to the lifetime of beginnings they've shared. Graduates drink to the challenge of work, while retirees drink to the challenge of avoiding it. A birthday toast counts the days that have passed, while a good-bye toast counts the days until we meet again. Your goal is to mark the occasion, no matter what it might be. *Toasts for Any Occasion* will help you make a fine toast, a wise toast, a funny toast, and a memorable toast. With a glass in one hand and this book in the other, a great toast is just a "Salut!" away.

To toasts!

WEDDINGS, ANNIVERSARIES, AND ROMANCE

HERE'S TO ROMANCE and to love.

Here's to a match made up above.

LOOK DOWN, you gods,

And on this couple drop a blessed crown.

—WILLIAM SHAKESPEARE, *The Tempest*

HERE'S TO HAPPINESS: May it fill your life always!

HERE'S TO differences:
An optimist's glass is half empty,
A pessimist's is half full, he knows.
A woman prefers to use crystal,
While a man will drink right from a hose.

MAY ALL YOUR TROUBLES be little ones,
And may you both live in love and happiness
For all the days of your lives.

—TRADITIONAL IRISH BLESSING

I'M SO GLAD the two of you found each other.
May you never be lost again.

A WEDDING DAY BEGINS with the beautiful sunrise
of joyful anticipation. May it end with the glorious sunset
of fulfilled promises.

IT IS NOT ENOUGH to wish you happiness in your life together.
I wish for you a lifetime of days even happier than today.

Two souls with but a single thought,

Two hearts that beat as one.

—Friedrich Halm

To the Groom: May you always remember how lucky you are to

be married to such an amazing woman.

To the Bride: May you always remain as radiant and full of hope

as you seem when gazing upon your new husband.

Matrimony—the high sea for which no compass

has yet been invented!

—Heinrich Heine

LET ALL THY JOYS be as the month of May,

And all thy days be as a marriage day:

Let sorrow, sickness, and a troubled mind

Be stranger to thee.

—FRANCIS QUARLES

MAY THIS couple

forever be blessed

With all that makes them

happiest!

MAY THE FLOWER OF LOVE never be nipped by the frost of disappointment, nor the shadow of grief fall upon you.

—TRADITIONAL IRISH BLESSING

YOU WAITED A WHILE to find each other, but that only proves good things are worth waiting for. To a long life together.

WHAT GREATER THING is there for two human souls than to feel that they are joined for all life—to strengthen each other in all labor, to rest on each other in all sorrow, to minister to each other in all pain, to be one with each other in silent unspeakable memories at the moment of the last parting?

—GEORGE ELIOT

HERE'S TO LOVE—
there is nothing warmer,
nothing sweeter,
nothing more beautiful.
May it always make you smile
and fill your hearts
with magic!

MAY YOUR CHILDREN grow up to look as beautiful and
as handsome as you do now, and may they never see your
high school graduation pictures.

NOTHING IS BETTER than good old-fashioned love.
May yours see a ripe old age.

HERE'S TO THE BRIDE: May your friends get married soon so you
can pass on some of the slow cookers you received today.
HERE'S TO THE GROOM: You've displayed wisdom we never
realized you had in choosing to give up bachelorhood for
your lovely new wife.

A TOAST TO THE BRIDE AND GROOM: May your love grow with
each passing day as you create the life of your dreams.

LOVE IS PATIENT, love is kind. It does not envy, it does not boast,

it is not proud. It is not rude, it is not self-seeking,

it is not easily angered, it keeps no record of wrongs.

Love does not delight in evil but rejoices with the truth.

It always protects, always trusts, always hopes, always perseveres.

—I Corinthians 13:4–7, NIV

MAY YOUR TROUBLES be less

And your blessings be more

And nothing but happiness come through your door.

—Traditional Irish Blessing

To LAUGHTER and caring

To love without end—

May you always be partners,

Lovers, and friends!

HERE'S TO the ABCs of marriage:

Always share everything

Be courteous

Communicate without kicking, screaming, or whining.

ALWAYS eat together.

Always sleep together.

Always be together.

BLESS THIS MARRIAGE, pure and strong.

Make it last a lifetime long.

WITH EACH DAY may you find something new to love

about one another.

YOU CAN'T BE EVERYTHING to anyone—except your spouse.

A toast to husbands and wives!

MAY YOUR WEDDING DAY be just the beginning of a new life overflowing with warmth, laughter, connection, friendship, hope, and love.

IF LIFE IS A DECK OF CARDS, the two of you are the king and queen of hearts—and I'm the joker who should have spent more time thinking about this toast.

YOU MAY laugh
You may cry
but may you always do it at each other's side.

To romance, to friendship, to affection, and to everything that connects the two of you and brings your lives together as one. To your life, to the future, and to your endless love.

To a love that grows ever stronger, ever closer. To a once-in-a-lifetime, forever love.

To friendship, love, and lots of babies!

CONGRATULATIONS TO THE HAPPY COUPLE. *And now it's time to eat, drink, and be married!*

GROW OLD ALONG with me!
The best is yet to be,
The last of life, for which the first is made.

—ROBERT BROWNING

A TOAST TO THIS AMAZING COUPLE, an example of the kind of deep love and friendship everyone dreams of— two people made for each other. Happy anniversary!

DRINK TO ME ONLY with thine eyes,
And I will pledge with mine;
Or leave a kiss within the cup
And I'll not look for wine.

—BEN JONSON

I LOVE THEE to the level of everyday's
Most quiet need, by sun and candle-light.
I love thee freely, as men strive for Right;
I love thee purely, as they turn from Praise.
I love thee with the passion put to use
In my old griefs, and with my childhood's faith.

—ELIZABETH BARRETT BROWNING

TO A COUPLE WHO HAVE always made love and marriage look so easy and natural. You two are the greatest—a perfect match!

HERE'S TO LOVING, to romance, to us.
May we travel together through time.
We alone count as none, but together we're one,
For our partnership puts love to rhyme.
—TRADITIONAL IRISH BLESSING

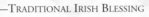

TO THE FATHER OF THE BRIDE: You're not losing a daughter,
you're gaining a bathroom, closet space, and a chance to finally
make bank deposits instead of withdrawals.

MAY THIS BE the first of endless expressions
of your love for one another.

LIFE LOOKS KINDLY on those who love and bestows special blessings on those who join their hearts. To both of you.

MAY YOU BE POOR in misfortune, rich in blessing,
slow to make enemies, quick to make friends.
But rich or poor, quick or slow,
may you know nothing but happiness from this day forward.

—TRADITIONAL IRISH BLESSING

A TOAST TO MY INSPIRATION, my hope—to the one who touches my heart so deeply, who knows me so completely. A toast to you—my soul mate and my one and only.

BIRTHDAYS, BIRTHS, AND ADOPTIONS

MAY ANGELS GUIDE you through the coming year and help you follow the path of your heart. Happy birthday to you!

TO BIRTHDAYS: Their importance is not how many you've had but rather how well you've celebrated.

MAY YOU LIVE all the days of your life.

—JONATHAN SWIFT

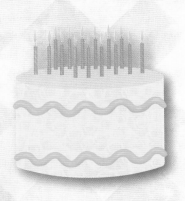

*Birthdays often have a negative connotation.
But when I look at you today and everything you've accomplished,
I can't help but wonder why birthdays are not met
with more optimism. You are truly an inspiration.
To you on your birthday.*

29

MAY GOD GRANT YOU many years to live,

For surely he must be knowing

The earth has angels all too few

And heaven's overflowing!

—TRADITIONAL IRISH BLESSING

TO A FRIEND who doesn't look any older than the day we met. And to my optician, who fitted me with rose-colored glasses.

TO SOMEONE WHO HAS outsmarted the numbers.

Age looks good on you.

MAY YOUR BIRTHDAY make you feel as beautiful and special

as you are.

YOU TOUCH THE LIVES and hearts of everyone you meet.

Happy birthday to someone who means so much to so many!

HERE'S TO ALL OF US—because we are so very lucky to

be counted among your friends!

WHAT THOUGH YOUTH gave love and roses,

Age still leaves us friends and wine.

—THOMAS MOORE

BIRTHDAYS ARE LIKE therapy sessions:
Everyone can tell when you've skipped a few.
Happy birthday anyway.

TO MIDDLE AGE, when everything you eat
goes to your middle.

GOD GRANT YOU many and happy years,
Till when the last has crowned you
The dawn of endless day appears,
And heaven is shining round you!

—OLIVER WENDELL HOLMES

EACH YEAR, you don't get older—you get more and more amazing!
More incredible! Here's to aging gracefully.

MAY YOU LIVE to be a hundred years with one extra to repent!
—TRADITIONAL IRISH BLESSING

HAPPY BIRTHDAY TO ONE who shines with happiness and so
readily shares it. May your day be as happy as you make others.

MAY YOU BE inspired by the clean slate of a brand new year.

birthday cake

MAY YOUR AGE be what every golfer wants: a good lie.

YOU'RE only as old as you feel,

And you look like you're feeling just great.

But we don't believe you're 29,

When you've got clothes that are 38.

34

BLESS OUR little ones today;
Bid your angels close to stay.
Protect them, Lord, as all the while
We see you in each sweet smile.

MAY YOUR NEW LITTLE ONE be as healthy and happy as
he [or she] *is beautiful!*

A NEW BABY IS God's greatest gift—until she [or he]
becomes a teenager! Then you know the wrath of God.
To the good years until then.

I DON'T KNOW WHO is more lucky—you for finding and adopting the perfect child or your new little baby who has been blessed with wonderful parents. To the new family!

THERE IS ONLY ONE pretty child in the world, and every mother has it.

—CHINESE PROVERB

MAY GOD BLESS your baby with his guidance on this baptism day and bless your family with his love.

BUSINESS—RETIREMENTS AND PROMOTIONS

HERE'S TO YOU: You're going to be great as a retired person—

after all, you've been practicing doing nothing for years!

TO A RARE and delightful person—and a job well done!

YESTERDAY WAS hard work and dedication.

Today is recognition and thanks.

Tomorrow is relaxation and fun.

It seems the best is yet to come.

MAY YOU FIND RETIREMENT like you found work: interesting, challenging, and a good way to kill time until happy hour.

THE DAILY GRIND for you now means lots of travel, long hours on the beach, and lunch breaks that last all afternoon. Enjoy!

BUSINESS BROUGHT US TOGETHER, but friendship has kept us close. Here's to you, a wonderful associate and friend!

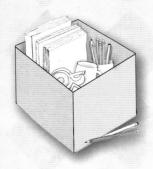

LEARN TO LIVE WELL, or fairly make your will;

You've played, and loved, and ate, and drank your fill:

Walk sober off; before a sprightlier age

Comes tittering on, and shoves you from the stage;

Leave such to trifle with more grace and ease,

Where folly pleases, and whose follies please.

—ALEXANDER POPE

We sure hope you saved money
For your retirement day,
Because we paid for this party
With your 401(k)!

Now that you've retired, we don't know what we'll do
without you—other than eat doughnuts, drink coffee,
and talk about Sunday's football game by ourselves.

Enjoy your retirement. Someone new may sit at your desk,
but no one will ever take your place!

WE'RE SURE SAD to see you go—and jealous, too!
Here's to you and your well-deserved retirement!

THE TIME TO BE happy is now.
The place to be happy is here.

—ROBERT G. INGERSOLL

HERE'S TO THE PAST—to a job well done.
Here's to the future—may you find it fulfilling, relaxing,
and filled with special moments that make you smile.

YOU'VE EARNED THE RIGHT to sleep in late
And dress a little sloppier
But please, can we still call you
When somebody jams our copier?

WE'RE GLAD YOU'RE HAPPY about retiring,
but we'd appreciate if you stopped referring to
your last paycheck as the Emancipation Proclamation.
May you enjoy your freedom.

HERE'S TO A MAN who spent 30 years doing what he loved—
and never got caught by his boss while he was doing it.

THE GREAT THING in this world is not so much where we stand,

as in what direction we are moving: To reach the port of heaven,

we must sail sometimes with the wind and sometimes against it,—

but we must sail, and not drift, nor lie at anchor.

—OLIVER WENDELL HOLMES

EVEN THOUGH WE HATE to do it, it's time to say good-bye.

There's so much about you we're going to miss—

not just the work you did, but your friendship and humor.

Here's to a colleague and a friend!

HAVING HAD THE PRIVILEGE to know you and work with you,
the main thing we want to say to you as you retire is:
Behave yourself!

THE ONLY THING more impressive than your long,
successful work history... is your agenda for retirement.

MAY YOUR RETIREMENT YEARS be happy,
Never boring or grotesque.
May you always have a smile on your face
Like when you slept at your desk.

THERE ARE SOME PEOPLE who just stand out,
for their loyalty, their dedication, their hard work.
Here's to a truly stand-out employee:
You are appreciated!

MAY YOU LOVE YOUR NEW JOB of being retired.
And may you be as good at it as you were at your job here!

DOST THOU LOVE LIFE? Then do not squander Time;
for that's the stuff life is made of.

—BENJAMIN FRANKLIN

YOU'RE MOVING UP, and nobody deserves it more. You've worked so very hard for this, and you're going to be absolutely great in your new position! To the future!

HERE'S TO SOMEONE who's definitely on the way up. May the journey be smooth, rewarding, and even a little bit fun! Congratulations!

LET'S TOAST to a well-deserved corner office!

YOU'RE ON a one-way road straight to the top.
Here's to reaching your goal.

GOOD LUCK AT YOUR NEW JOB, and thank you for all your
accomplishments here. Savor them as you look to the future.

I HOPE YOU'RE NOT afraid of heights,
because I have a feeling your journey upward
has just begun.

IT'S HARD TO LOSE YOU—
you've been such a terrific employee—
but it's always great to see someone who works so hard
moving on and up. Here's wishing you the very best of luck
in your new job!

CONGRATULATIONS ON YOUR PROMOTION,
and always remember the people who worked hard
to help you get it. And then remember us:
the people who surfed the Internet so you didn't have
much competition for it.

GRADUATIONS

THE WORLD IS a lucky place to have you coming its way.

Congratulations!

⟐

HAVE MORE than thou showest,
Speak less than thou knowest,
Lend less than thou owest.

—WILLIAM SHAKESPEARE

⟐

A TOAST TO ANTICIPATION of all that lies before you.

A toast to the celebration of all that you have accomplished.

A toast to you—the graduate!

ALWAYS REACH FOR THE STARS, and they will meet your grasp,

for you are hope and light and the promise of the future.

Congratulations!

APPLY THE SAME PASSION, purpose, and power to
your dreams as you have to your education,
and nothing will be impossible for you to achieve.
To what lies ahead!

TO THE glad grad!

HERE'S TO the graduate
And to the diploma that you have earned.
Welcome to the real world
Where you may forget everything you learned.

YOU'VE WORKED SO VERY HARD to get to this moment.
May the future bring you all the rewards you so richly deserve.

AS A CHILD, you probably had dozens of ideas for what you wanted
to be when you grew up. Now you're educated and capable of
making your own decisions. "Eeeny, Meeny, Miney, Mo…"

ONLY THE educated are free.

—EPICTETUS

MAY YOUR EDUCATION bring you many degrees of
happiness and accomplishment.

*MAY YOU NEVER STOP LEARNING as you leave
the halls of education. May you never stop achieving in the greatest
school of all—the school of life.*

*HERE'S TO THE BEST NEWS a graduate can receive:
There is no such thing as your permanent record.*

*THE PAST IS BUT THE BEGINNING of a beginning, and . . .
all that is and has been is but the twilight of the dawn.*

—H. G. WELLS

THE POSSIBILITIES BEFORE YOU now are like the ocean.

There is nothing left to do but dive in.

LEARNING IS A TREASURE,

which accompanies its owner everywhere.

—CHINESE PROVERB

LET NOT YOUR EDUCATION end here. Be a beacon of hope for others struggling to reach the place where you proudly stand today. For you now hold the power to motivate, to inspire, to encourage. No longer the student, you become the teacher.

CONGRATULATIONS!

You've moved one step up the ladder of life!

HERE'S TO HEALTH in homely rhyme

To our oldest classmate, Father Time;

May our last survivor live to be

As bold and wise and as thorough as he!

—OLIVER WENDELL HOLMES

HOLIDAYS

NEW YEAR'S DAY

BE AT WAR with your vices,

At peace with your neighbours,

And let every New Year find you a better man.

—BENJAMIN FRANKLIN

TO GOOD HEALTH, success, and friendship in the new year.

EASTER

TO THE TRUE SPIRIT and meaning of Easter,
to remembering that he died for us.
We owe it to him and to ourselves to live our lives
in a way that reflects upon his goodness and love and
that is worthy of his sacrifice.
Happy Easter!

HERE'S TO EASTER—and the emerging spring. May this be a time
of renewal for this green earth and for each of us.

April Fool's Day

Let us be thankful for the fools.
But for them the rest of us could not succeed.

—Mark Twain

Mother's Day

Mom, this day is a day for you, a day to do something
we all too often forget to do, and that's to say,
"Thank you, Mom—you're the best!"

To mothers everywhere.
They give us life, but they continue giving to make sure
our lives are worthwhile. Our first relationship is with our mother,
and in many ways it remains our best.

Father's Day

Dad, there's no other way to say it: You're awesome!
You're loved! And here's to you, Dad!

As a child, I thought he was the wisest, most decent man
I'd ever known. As an adult, my opinion hasn't changed.
A toast to my father!

FOURTH OF JULY

HERE'S TO A GREAT and proud country, a country where freedom is prized above all else. Here's to our country: Our heartland, our home. God bless America!

ONE FLAG, ONE LAND, one heart, one hand. One Nation evermore!

—OLIVER WENDELL HOLMES

TO OUR FOREBEARS, who spent their lives building this country. To all who have served and given their lives for this country. To the United States of America: home of the brave and land of the free!

THANKSGIVING

HERE'S TO OUR LIVES—we are so rich in
family and friends.
Let us lift our glasses in thanksgiving!

LET US OFFER OUR GRATITUDE that we are gathered together here
today and share our wish that everyone may be as blessed as we are!

THANKSGIVING IS A TIME for giving thanks.
That's why I want to thank all of you for making my life
such a blessing. To all who share our table.

CHRISTMAS

MAY THE MAGIC AND WONDER of Christmas bless this home and bring you peace in the New Year.

I HEARD THE BELLS on Christmas Day

Their old, familiar carols play,

And wild and sweet

The words repeat

Of peace on earth, good-will to men.

—HENRY WADSWORTH LONGFELLOW

GOD BLESS US every one!

—TINY TIM'S TOAST IN *A CHRISTMAS CAROL* BY CHARLES DICKENS

INTERNATIONAL OCCASIONS

MAY THE ROAD RISE to meet you,
May the wind be always at your back,
The sun shine warmly upon your face,
The rain fall soft upon your fields,
And until we meet again may God hold you in
the hollow of his hand.

—IRELAND

I RAISE MY GLASS to wish you your heart's desire.

—RUSSIA

May the Lord keep you in the palm of his hand,
And never close his fist too tight upon you.

—IRELAND

Eis Igian!

—GREECE

Noroc!

—ROMANIA

BREAD TO FEED our friendship,

Salt to keep it true,

Water is for a welcome,

And wine to drink with you.

—FRANCE

MAZEL TOV!

—YIDDISH CONGRATULATIONS

MAY BAD FORTUNE follow you all your days and

never catch up!

—IRELAND

VIVA L'AMOR!

—ITALY

SKAL!

—SWEDEN

MAY THE SAINTS protect you,
And sorrow neglect you,
And bad luck to the one
That doesn't respect you.

—IRELAND

A la sature!

—INDIA

Za zdorovia!

—RUSSIA

May you have warm words on a cold evening,
A full moon on a dark night,
And the road downhill all the way to your door.

—IRELAND

KEDVES egeszsegere!

—HUNGARY

MAY THE WINDS of adversity ne'er blow open our door.

—SCOTLAND

OP UW gezonheid!

—BELGIUM

L'CHAIM!

—ISRAEL

FEE SIHETAK!

—EGYPT

HERE'S TO absent friends,
And here's twice to absent enemies.

—IRELAND

KAMPAI!

—JAPAN

PROSIT!

—GERMANY

MAY YOU HAVE FOOD and raiment,
A soft pillow for your head,
May you be 40 years in heaven
Before the devil knows you're dead.

—IRELAND

KONG GANG ul wi ha yo!

—KOREA

HERE'S TO A SWEETHEART, a bottle, and a friend.
The first beautiful, the second full, the last ever faithful.

—IRELAND

A VORTRE sante!

—FRANCE

MAY YOUR RIGHT HAND always be stretched out in friendship,
But never in want.

—IRELAND

OTHER OCCASIONS AND THEMES

FRIENDSHIP

WERE IT THE LAST DROP in the well,

As I gasp'd upon the brink,

E're my fainting spirit fell,

'Tis to thee that I would drink.

—LORD BYRON, TO HIS FRIEND TOM MOORE

HERE'S TO A TRUE FRIEND who's seen my good side and my bad side and always invites both to the party.

IN MATTER of style,
Swim with the currents.
In matter of principle,
Stand like a rock.

—THOMAS JEFFERSON

DO ALL THE GOOD you can,
By all the means you can,
In all the ways you can,
At all the times you can,
To all the people you can,
As long as ever you can.

—JOHN WESLEY

GOOD COMPANY, good wine, good welcome
Can make good people.

—WILLIAM SHAKESPEARE

DRINKING

AND FILL THEM HIGH with generous juice,
As generous as your mind,
And pledge me in the generous toast,
The whole of humankind!

—ROBERT BURNS

He who clinks his cup with mine,

Adds a glory to the wine.

—George Sterling

If all be true as we do think,

There are five reasons why we drink,

Good wine, a friend, or being dry,

Or lest one should be, by and by,

Or any other reason why!

—Henry Aldrich

COME FILL A FLOWING BOWL until it does run over,

Tonight we will all merry be,

Tomorrow we'll get sober.

—JOHN FLETCHER

EAT THY BREAD with joy,

And drink thy wine with a merry heart.

—ECCLESIASTES 9:7, KJV

HEALTH

HERE'S TO YOUR GOOD HEALTH, and your family's good health,
and may you all live long and prosper.

—WASHINGTON IRVING

GOOD-BYE

IT'S SO HARD TO SAY GOOD-BYE, but so easy to say "Good luck."